The Dilemma of a Ghost

KU-525-437

African Creative Writing Series

General Editor: Michael J.C. Echeruo,
Professor of English,
University of Ibadan

The Dilemma of a Ghost

Ama Ata Aidoo

Longman

LONGMAN GROUP LIMITED
LONDON

Associated companies, branches and
representatives throughout the world

© C.A.A. Aidoo 1965

All rights reserved. No part of this
publication may be reproduced, stored
in a retrieval system, or transmitted
in any form or by any means, electronic,
mechanical, photocopying, recording, or
otherwise, without the prior permission
of the Copyright owner.

First published 1965
ACWS edition 1977

ISBN 0 582 60836 8

Printed in Hong Kong by
The Hong Kong Printing Press (1977) Ltd

TO THE MEMORY OF PAAPA,
WITH THANKS FOR EVERYTHING

CHARACTERS

ATO YAWSON: [Ebow] *A young Ghanaian graduate*
EULALIE YAWSON (*née* RUSH): *Afro-American graduate*
ESI KOM: [Maami] *Ato's mother*

MONKA: *His sister*
NANA: *His grandmother*
AKYERE: *His elder aunt*
MANSA: *His younger aunt*
PETU: *His elder uncle*
AKROMA: *His younger uncle*

1ST WOMAN } *Neighbours*
2ND WOMAN }

BOY } *Two children in a dream. The boy being the*
GIRL } *ghost of Ato's former self*

The Bird of the Wayside

The Dilemma of a Ghost was first presented by the Students' Theatre, Legon, on the 12th, 13th and 14th of March, 1964, at the Open-Air Theatre, Commonwealth Hall, University of Ghana, Legon

The action takes place in the courtyard of the newest wing of the Odumna Clan house. It is enclosed on the right by a wall of the old building and both at the centre and on the left by the walls of the new wing. At the right-hand corner a door links the courtyard with a passage that leads into the much bigger courtyard of the old house. In the middle of the left wall there is a door leading into the new rooms. A terrace runs round the two sides of the new sector.

In the foreground is the path which links the roads leading to the river, the farm and the market.

PRELUDE

I am the Bird of the Wayside –
The sudden scampering in the undergrowth,
Or the trunkless head
Of the shadow in the corner.
I am an asthmatic old hag
Eternally breaking the nuts
Whose soup, alas,
Nourished a bundle of whitened bones –
Or a pair of women, your neighbours
Chattering their lives away.
I can furnish you with reasons why
This and that and other things
Happened. But stranger,
What would you have me say
About the Odumna Clan? . . .
Look around you,
For the mouth must not tell everything.
Sometimes the eye can see
And the ear should hear.
Yonder house is larger than
Any in the town –
Old as the names
Oburumankuma, Odapadjan, Osun.
They multiply faster than fowls
And they acquire gold
As if it were corn grains –
But if in the making of
One Scholar
Much is gone
You stranger do not know.

Just you listen to their horn-blower:
'We came from left
We came from right
We came from left
We came from right
The twig shall not pierce our eyes
Nor the rivers prevail o'er us.
We are of the vanguard
We are running forward, forward, forward . . .'

Thus, it is only to be expected that they should reserve the new addition to the house for the exclusive use of the One Scholar. Not that they expect him to make his home there. No . . . he will certainly have to live and work in the city when he arrives from the white man's land.

But they all expect him to come down, now and then, at the weekend and on festive occasions like Christmas. And certainly, he must come home for blessings when the new yam has been harvested and the Stools are sprinkled. The ghosts of the dead ancestors are invoked and there is no discord, only harmony and a restoration of that which needs to be restored. But the Day of Planning is different from the Day of Battle. And when the One Scholar came . . . I cannot tell you what happened. You shall see that anon. But it all began on a University Campus; never mind where. The evening was cool as evenings are. Darkness was approaching when I heard the voices of a man and woman speaking . . .

EU: Graduation! Ah well, that too isn't bad. But who's a graduate? What sort of creature is it? Why should I have supposed that mere graduation is a passport to happiness?

ATO: [*Harshly*] If you must know, woman, I think you do get on my nerves. Since you do not think much of a degree, why for heaven's sake did you go in for it?

EU: Don't shout at me, if you please.

ATO: Do keep your mouth shut, if you please.

EU: I suppose African women don't talk?

ATO: How often do you want to drag in about African women?

Leave them alone, will you . . . Ah yes they talk. But Christ, they don't run on in this way. This running-tap drawl gets on my nerves.

EU: What do you mean?

ATO: I mean exactly what I said.

EU: Look here, I don't think that I'll stand by and have you say I am not as good as your folks.

ATO: But what have I said, for goodness sake?

EU: Well, what did you mean by running-tap drawl? I only speak like I was born to speak – like an American!

ATO: [*Contrite*] Nonsense, darling . . . But Sweetie Pie, can't we ever talk, but we must drag in the differences between your people and mine? Darling, we'll be happy, won't we?

EU: [*Relaxing*] I'm optimistic, Native Boy. To belong to somewhere again . . . Sure, this must be bliss.

ATO: Poor Sweetie Pie.

EU: But I will not be poor again, will I? I'll just be 'Sweetie Pie'. Waw! The palm trees, the azure sea, the sun and golden beaches . . .

ATO: Steady, woman. Where did you get hold of a tourist brochure? There are no palms where we will live. There are coconut trees . . . coconut palms, though. Unless of course if I take you to see my folks at home. There are real palm trees there.

EU: Ah well, I don't know the difference, and I don't care neither. Coconut palms, palm-palms, aren't they all the same? And anyway, why should I not go and see your folks?

ATO: You may not be impressed.

EU: Silly darling. Who wants to be impressed? Fine folks Eulalie Rush has herself, eh? Could I even point to you a beggar in the streets as my father or mother? Ato, can't your Ma be sort of my Ma too?

ATO: [*Slowly and uncertainly*] Sure she can.

EU: And your Pa mine?

ATO: Sure.

3

[*Following lines solemn, like a prayer*]

And all my people your people . . .

EU: And your gods my gods?

ATO: Yes.

EU: Shall I die where you will die?

ATO: Yes . . . And if you want to, you shall be buried there also.
[*Pause*]

EU: [*Anxiously*] But darling, I really hope it won't matter at all?

ATO: What?

EU: You know what, Native Boy.

ATO: 'Lalie, don't you believe me when I tell you it's O.K.? I
love you, Eulalie, and that's what matters. Your own sweet
self should be O.K. for any guy. And how can a first-born
child be difficult to please? Children, who wants them? In
fact, they will make me jealous. I couldn't bear seeing you
love someone else better than you do me. Not yet, darling,
and not even my own children.

EU: You really sure?

ATO: Aren't you the sweetest and loveliest things in Africa and
America rolled together? My darling, we are going to
create a paradise, with or without children.

EU: Darling, some men do mind a lot.

ATO: [*Vehemently*] Look at me, we shall postpone having children
for as long you would want.

EU: But still, I understand in Africa . . .

ATO: . . . Eulalie Rush and Ato Yawson shall be free to love each
other, eh? This is all that you understand or should understand about Africa.

EU: [*Delighted*] Silly, I wasn't going to say that.

ATO: Then forget about what you were going to say.

EU: [*Persistently*] I only hope it's O.K.

ATO: It shall be O.K.

EU: Ato!

ACT ONE

Evening. The two village women are returning from the river with their water pots on their heads.

1ST W: Ah! And yet I thought I was alone in this . . .
        The lonely woman who must toil
        From morn till eve,
        Before a morsel hits her teeth
        Or a drop of water cools her throat.
2ND W: My sister, you are not alone.
        But who would have thought that I,
        Whose house is teeming with children,
        My own, my husband's, my sister's . . .
        But this is my curse.
        'Shall I do this when
        This and that have nothing to do?'
        No. And they all sit
        With their hands between their knees.
        If the courtyard must be swept,
        It is Aba's job.
        If the *ampesi* must be cooked,
        It is Aba's job.
        And since the common slave was away all day
        There was no drop in the pot
        To cool the parched throat.
        I am telling you, my sister,
        Sometimes we feel you are luckier
        Who are childless.
1ST W: But at the very last
        You are luckiest who have them.
        Take Esi Kom, I say.

        [ESI KOM *enters from the door on the right with two stools*

B

which she puts on the centre of the stage. For the rest of the scene, she moves stealthily but swiftly in and out of the stage arranging six stools in preparation for the next scene.]

2ND W: What has happened?

1ST W: You know her son
That was away beyond the seas
Is now come back?

2ND W: So, that explains the new paint. When?

1ST W: Yesternight.

2ND W: Is he here?

1ST W: I do not know.

2ND W: I heard her younger children
Crying for eggs.

1ST W: Which means that those of us
Who are in this neighbourhood
Are going to have our mouths watering
With the aroma of the fryings and stewings.

2ND W: Of course, that is what she always does.
And meanwhile the debts pile up.

1ST W: Yes, but the arrival of the son
May mean the paying of all the debts at last.
Her soul is a good one.

2ND W: Hmm. For my part, I would be ashamed
To live in a Clan house for
As long as she has done.
But let us hurry, my sister
For my food is getting cold.

[*They go out. After a minute or so, ESI KOM goes out too, having finished arranging the stools.*]

. . . . .

[*Later. It is quite dark now. The old woman totters in supported by her stick. In her youth, she had been a short, dark petite femme with a will like iron. Now, though she is weak, her tongue is as sharp if not sharper for her eighty plus. She sits on one of the stools in the centre of the stage. She props her chin on her stick. Presently* ATO *enters from the door on the left. For a few seconds the old woman continues sitting motionless as if she has not seen him, then suddenly she speaks.*]

NANA: I am glad you came and found me alive.

ATO: I am glad too.

NANA: And what is on your mind, my grandson.

ATO: There is nothing else on my mind, Nana.

NANA: Were you not thinking, nay hoping, you will come and find me dead?

ATO: Oh!

NANA: Do not be pained my grand-child. I just wanted to trouble you a little. But go and tell your mother that if she and the others do not come early, I will be angry. [ATO *leaves by the door on the right.*] Already, naughty slumber is stealing over my senses. [*A clanging noise from within.*] Yes, someone has tripped in the doorway, eh. One day the people in this house will commit murder. Do they not know that if the heavens withdraw their light, man must light his own way? But no. They will let us all lie in darkness. How will he find his way around this dark place should the ghost of one of our forebearers pay us a visit? But this is something one should not speak about. They say they buy *kresin* and pay for it with money . . . ah, as if the penny will shine and light our way when it is tied in a cloth . . . But of course, they will say I talk too much . . . Are they not coming? They are now removing their pans, tchia! Are these women? I shit upon such women. When we were young, a woman cleared her eating place after the last morsel had hardly touched her tongue. But now, they will allow their noise-making pans to lie around for people to trip over. But it is not their fault. If they had to use earthenware pots which broke more easily than eggs, they would have learnt their lessons long ago.

ATO: [*From within*] Maami, why do not you and my Uncles hurry? Nana is getting impatient. [*He re-enters.*]

NANA: Have your Uncles Petu and Akroma come?

ATO: Yes, Nana. [*Voices from within.*]

MANSA: [*From within*] Oh, the old woman again!

NANA: Are those speaking your aunts?

ATO: Yes, Nana.

NANA: But what are they doing there?

[*Several voices.* PETU *and* AKROMA *come in. The two men sit down.*]

PETU: Old woman, we greet you.

NANA: I respond, my Royal Ones. And how are you?

PETU: We are all well, Old One.

[ATO *slips into his room, left*]

NANA: Akroma, how is your wife's stomach?

AKROMA: It is a bit better.

NANA: I notice you do not feel clear in your own inside. You people always say I talk too much. So I try not to put my tongue in your affairs. But I hope you would think of what I always say. Have we not had enough of the white man's medicines? Since they do not seem to do anything for your wife, why do you not take her to Kofikrom? The herbalist there is famous . . .

AKROMA: I have heard you, Old One. I would put it to her people and hear what they have got to say too.

NANA: [*With her eyes turned towards the entrance*] I say, what are you doing there? Why are you doing this thing to me?

FEMALE VOICES: Ah, here we are. [ESI KOM, AKYERE *and* MANSA *enter. The stage is well-lit now. The women sit around on the terrace.*]

NANA: Ah, your characters are not pleasing. What were you really doing by the hearth. I thought you know that I must not sit here until the dew falls on me.

MANSA: Old One, it is all right. We won't do this again.

AKROMA: But where is our master, the white man himself?

ATO: [*From within*] I am coming, Uncle. [*He comes out.*]

PETU: But where are you sitting? . . .

ESI: [*Overlapping* PETU *and directing her voice to the old sector*] Monka, are you not bringing your brother a chair?

MONKA: [*From within*] *Hei* Ebow!

ALL: What is it?

MONKA: [*Coming back with a chair*] The way some people become scholars is fearful.

ATO: What is the matter?

MONKA: The master scholar was sitting on the chair studying, so he could not move off! [ATO *laughs.*] After all, what is he learning? Is it the knowledge of the leopard skin? [*Sucks her teeth.*]

ESI: If it had been in any other home, he, Ebow, would have seen to it that we were all seated.

AKROMA: But I do not know what he has done for all of you to pick on him in this way.

ESI: Let us say what we cannot keep in us any longer, for the day Ebow becomes like you, he will kick us all around as if we were his footballs.

NANA: Esi Kom, leave that child alone, for no one knows what the man of fame and honour was like when he was a child.

AKROMA: But Old One, we can soon know the bird which will not do well, for his nest hangs by the wayside.

ATO: Let us give him, too, some time.

MONKA: I always say that one can always know the man who is civilised.

NANA: I think you should all know that Ato was always a humble one.

PETU: Of course, he is a first born. Our eldest hold that first borns are always humble. Our white master, we welcome you.

ATO: I thank you, Uncle.

PETU: Ah, we have been here at home but you . . .

AKYERE: I say . . .

PETU: What is it?

AKYERE: I say, Esi. For a long time I have not been seeing that sheep which you were rearing in Ato's name.

AKROMA: As for you women.

ESI: Ho, I have sold it.

MANSA and AKYERE: Sold it!

ESI: But yes.

AKYERE: What did you do with the money?

ESI: [*Indirectly addressing* ATO] I have not done anything with it. It had a good market and I thought I would find some more money and add to it to give to Ato's father to pay for the bride price for its owner.

AKYERE: That is very good.

PETU: But women, can you not wait for us to finish what we came here to say? The child has just come from a journey. You have not welcomed him but already you want to marry for him.

ATO: [*As if just awake from sleep*] Ei, Uncle, are you talking of marriage?

ESI: It is nothing. I was only telling your aunt that I have sold your sheep to pay the bride price for you when you make up your mind to marry . . .

ATO: [*Casually*] But I am already married, Maami.

ALL: You are married? Married! Married!

ESI: [*Overlapping*] Who is your wife?

AKYERE: [*Overlapping*] When did you marry?

MANSA: Who is your wife?

MONKA: [*Overlapping*] What is her name?

ESI: Where does she come from?

[*Everyone repeats her words to create confusion.*]

PETU: You must all be quiet. One must take time to dissect an ant in order to discover its entrails.

MONKA: [*Laughing wickedly*] Ei, so I have a sister-in-law whom I do not know?

AKROMA: *Ei,* Monka, keep quiet.

NANA: [*Who has been sleeping since she last spoke*] What is all this noise about? Have you asked the child news from his journey?

[*Silence while everyone stares at* ATO.]

PETU: Ato, when did you marry?

ATO: That is what I was going to tell you. One week ago.

NANA: [*Spitting*] My grand-child, so you have married? Why did you never write to tell us.

ESI: Ato my son, who is your wife?

ATO: [*Quite embarrassed*] Eulalie.

ALL: Eh!

ATO: I said 'Eulalie'. [*By now all the women are standing.*]

MONKA: Hurere!

ESI: Petu! Akyere! What does he say?

THE W: Hurere!

MONKA: Oh, let us say, let us say that some of the names that are coming into the world are fearful.

ESI: Ato, you know that some of us did not hear the school bell when it rang. Therefore we will not be able to say this name. This Uhu-hu . . . I want her real name, my son.

ATO: But Maami, this is her only name.

MANSA: Our master, isn't your wife . . . eh . . . Fanti?

ATO: No, aunt.

AKYERE: [*Contemptuously*] If so, what is her tribe?

ATO: She has no tribe. She does not come from . . .

NANA: [*Looking up at him*] She has no tribe? The story you are telling us is too sweet, my grand-child. Since I was born, I have not heard of a human being born out from the womb of a woman who has no tribe. Are there trees which never have any roots?

PETU: Ato, where does your wife come from? [*A short silence. All look at* ATO.]

ATO: But no one is prepared to listen to me. My wife comes from . . . America.

ESI: [*Putting her hands on her head*] Oh Esi! You have an unkind soul. We always hear of other women's sons going to the white man's country. Why should my own go and marry a white woman?

MONKA: Amrika! My brother, you have arrived indeed.

AKYERE: But we thought that we too have found a treasure at last for our house. What have you done to us, my son? We do not know the ways of the white people. Will not people laugh at us?

ATO: [*Very nervously*] But who says I have married a white woman? Is everyone in America white? In that country there are white men and black men.

AKROMA: Nephew, you must tell us properly. We do not know.

ATO: But you will not listen to me. [*All quiet. Eyes are focused on* ATO.] I say my wife is as black as we all are. [*Sighs of relaxation.*]

ESI: But how is it, my child, that she comes from Amrika and she has this strange name? [*The old woman spits significantly.*]

NANA: Is that what people call their children in the white man's country?

ATO: [*Irritably*] It is not the white man's country.

ALL: O . . . O . . . Oh!

ATO: Please, I beg you all, listen. Eulalie's ancestors were of our ancestors. But [*warming up*] as you all know, the white people came and took some away in ships to be slaves . . .

NANA: [*Calmly*] And so, my grand-child, all you want to tell us is that your wife is a slave? [*At this point even the men get up with shock from their seats. All the women break into violent weeping.* ESI KOM *is beside herself with grief. She walks round in all attitudes of mourning.*]

ATO: [*Wildly*] But she is not a slave. It was her grandfathers and her grandmothers who were slaves.

NANA: Ato, do not talk with the foolishness of your generation.

[*The two village women come into the path.*]

1ST W: My sister, what can be the meaning of this?
2ND W: That is what I cannot see.
1ST W: Probably the old woman is dead.
2ND W: She has not been very well lately.
1ST W: This is life.
Some are going
While others are coming.
That is the road to the life hereafter.
2ND W: Then let us start weeping, my sister.

[*They begin to weep and walk up stage, then they notice*
NANA.]

1ST W: Ah, but look, she is sitting there.

NANA: [*Hobbles towards the women*] Yes, I am sitting here. So you
thought I was dead? No, I am not. Go home good neighbours and save your tears for my funeral. It cannot be long
now . . . Go.

[*The women turn back.*]

No, do not go yet. I still need your tears.
[*All eyes turned on the women.*] My grand-child has gone
and brought home the offspring of slaves. [*Women's faces
indicate horror.*] A slave, I say.

[ESI KOM *enacts horror and great distress.*]

Hear what has befallen our house.
ATO: [*Moving to the front of the stage*] Heavens! Is there any
reason why you should make so much fuss? All because I

have married an American Negro? If you only know how sweet Eulalie is! [*He looks at the women and whistles.*] Now all this racket you are putting on will bring the whole town here. [*He turns back abruptly, goes to his door, enters and closes it on the scene. All eyes are turned to the closed door now.*]

NANA: My spirit Mother ought to have come for me earlier.
Now what shall I tell them who are gone? The daughter of
slaves who come from the white man's land.
Someone should advise me on how to tell my story.
My children, I am dreading my arrival there
Where they will ask me news of home.
Shall I tell them or shall I not?
Someone should lend me a tongue
Light enough with which to tell
My Royal Dead
That one of their stock
Has gone away and brought to their sacred precincts
The wayfarer!

[*Everyone except* NANA *starts leaving the stage.*]

They will ask me where I was
When such things were happening.
O mighty God!
Even when the Unmentionable
Came and carried off the children of the house
In shoals like fish,
Nana Kum kept his feet steadfast on the ground
And refused to let any of his nephews
Take a wife from a doubtful stock.

[*She turns to leave, and walks towards the door on the right.*]

If it is true that the last gets the best of everything
Then what is this
Which my soul has drawn out for me?

[*Lights go out.*]

ACT TWO

[A fortnight later. Afternoon. The two village women are returning from the woods where they have gathered some faggots.]

2ND W: *Ei*, Esi Kom.
  Some child bearing is profitable.
1ST W: What has happened now?
2ND W: Nothing. It is only that I remember
  Her and her affairs when we pass their house.
1ST W: Child bearing is always profitable
  For were not our fathers wise
  Who looked upon the motion of our lives
  And said,
  They ask for the people of the house
  And not the money in it?
  There is nothing that can compare with
  Being a parent, my sister.
2ND W: Not always, my sister
  If you perchance hear on a silent afternoon
  The sound of a pestle hitting a mortar,
  Go get out your mortar too
  For they are only pounding cassava.
1ST W: Perchance they are pounding yam.
2ND W: Have you forgotten the daughter of this same
  Esi Kom? Have you not heard it whispered?
  Have you not heard it sung
  From the end of the East road
  To the beginning of the West
  That Monka never marries well?
1ST W: But if Esi Kom bears a daughter
  And the daughter finds no good man
  Shall we say
  It is Esi Kom's fate in childbirth,

Or shall we say it is her daughter's trouble?
Is not Monka the sauciest girl
Born here for many years?
Has she not the hardest mouth in this town?

2ND W: That is as it may
But Esi Kom suffers for it.

1ST W: My sister, even from bad marriages
Are born good sons and daughters.

2ND W: Who shall look after them?

1ST W: Do you ask that of me
When everybody knows
A son is back from the land beyond the seas?
Shall he not help to look after his nephews
And nieces when it was somebody else who
Looked after him in the days of his childhood?
You talk, my sister,
As if the days are gone
When the left hand washed the right
And the right hand washed the left.

2ND W: Perhaps they are not, my sister.
But those days are over
When it was expedient for two deer
To walk together,
Since anyone can see and remove
The beam in his eye with a mirror.

1ST W: These are sad sayings, my sister.
But where is his wife?

2ND W: I do not know, my sister.
But I heard them say that his mother
Had gone to knock the door of Yaw Mensa
To ask for the hand of his daughter for him.

1ST W: Oh, he would have had a good woman.
I saw that girl when she came home last Christmas.
School has not spoilt her, I think.

2ND W: And that is the sad part of it, my sister.
He has not taken this girl

17

Whom we all know and like,
But has gone for this
Black—white woman.
A stranger and a slave —
But that is his and Esi Kom's affair.
I hear in the distance the cry of a child
That cry is meant for my ear.
Let us hurry home, my sister.
[*She takes the lead.*]

1ST W: Oh, Eternal Mother Nature,
Queen Mother of childbirth,
How was it you went past my house
　　Without a pause
　　Without a rest?
Mighty God, when shall the cry of an infant
Come into my ear;
For the sun has journeyed far
In my sky.
[*Lights out.*]

*　　*　　*　　*

[*Late afternoon of the next day. Everywhere is quiet.* ATO *is asleep in the inner room.* EULALIE *comes in with a packet of cigarettes, a lighter, an ash tray and a bottle of Coca-Cola. She sits on the terrace facing the audience. She begins sipping the Coca-Cola and soon the voice of her mind comes across the courtyard. Later her mother's voice is also heard. As the voices speak on, her body relaxes except for her mouth which breaks into a light smile or draws up tightly; and her eyes, which stare in front of her or dart left and right generally expressing the emotions that her thoughts arouse in her.*] [*On the other hand the passage could be spoken as a soliloquy with the mother's voice interrupting from back stage.*]

VOICE: So at last here am I in Africa . . . Joseph and Mary! I hope

I've done the right thing. What good fun I'm going to have here! [*Smiles.*] Just reckon. I hear the cottons are exactly the thing! You hold on until I go to the shops . . . [*She starts as she hears a rumble of drums*] . . . And anyway, supposing this is just an ugly mess I've let myself into, what am I going to do? You got a heart, Eulalie Rush? No. Now it's over to you Eulalie Yawson . . . Yawson. That surely is a name. [*Smiles.*] Life can be funny at times, that's what Fiona used to say. Now, I must sort of confess that I am finding all this rather cute. Ato says there will be two boys in the house. Fiona, if you could only see me now. [*Mouth grim.*] Or is it rather if I could only see you now? Sometimes a girl would just like to have someone she loves and knows to tell things to and laugh with. But there is no one for me here who would have understood like you would, Fiona. There is no one even back in the States . . . Christ, Fiona, Pa and Ma! There was no one left was there? [*Bends her head.*] And how can one make a family out of Harlem? Ma . . . with her hands chapped with washing to keep me in College . . . I say [*Smiles*], I never knew there is Coke in these parts. [*Holding the Coca-Cola bottle affectionately.*] Fiona would have been shocked to hear it. How we used to talk of the jungle and the wild life . . . And I haven't seen a lion yet! As for his folks, they are cute. I adore the old one . . . His mother gives me a feeling, though. [*She starts and stares as she hears the drums again.*] Ma, I've come to the very source. I've come to Africa and I hope that where'er you are, you sort of know and approve. '"Lalie", you shall not stop. Chicken, you must have it all.' And I had it all, Ma, even graduation. 'You'll be swank enough to look a white trash in the eye and tell him to go to hell.' Ma, ain't I telling the whole of the States to go swing! Congress, Jew and white trash, from Manhattan to Harlem . . . 'Sugar, don't let them do you in.' Ma, I didn't. 'Sugar, don't sort of curse me and your Pa every morning you look your face in the mirror and see yourself black. Kill the sort of dreams silly girls dream that they are going to wake up one morning and find their skins milk white and their hairs soft blonde like them Hollywood tarts. Sugar, the dear God made you just that black and you canna do nothing about it.' Ma, it was hard not to dream but I tried . . . only I wish you were not dead . . . I wish you were right here, not even in the States, but here in this country where there will be no washing for you no more and where . . . where . . . Oh Ma! But I know you would pat me on the back and say, 'Sugar, you sure done fine.' Native Boy is the blackest you ever saw . . .

[*Suddenly the drums just roll and roll.* EULALIE *throws away her cigarette, her eyes pop out. She is really scared. She mutters 'Christ, Christ' like a caged animal. She rushes towards the room and crashes into Ato's arms.*]

ATO: Hullo, my sweet. [*Then he notices her frightened look.*] What is the matter?

EU: Can't you hear?

ATO: Ah, what is it?

EU: Can't you hear the drums?

ATO: [*Cocks his ears*] Oh, those!

EU: Aren't you afraid? I am.

ATO: Don't be absurd, darling. [*Holds her close.*] But I thought that one thing which attracted you about Africa was that there is a lot of drumming here.

EU: [*Relaxes and thinks*] Y – e – s. But, you know, I didn't guess they'll be sort of like this.

ATO: You thought they would sound like jazz?

EU: Sure. Or rather like, you know, sort of Spanish mambo.

ATO: I see. [*Chuckles.*] But there is nothing specially frightening about this, is there?

EU: I don't know. I only thought it was witch-hunting.

ATO: What?

EU: Witch-hunting.

ATO: Witch . . . [*He bursts out laughing till he is quite breathless.*] Witch-hunting? O mine, who put that idea into your head?

EU: But I understand there is always witch-hunting out here in Africa.

ATO: But still, why were you so scared? You aren't a witch yourself, are you?

EU: Don't tease.

ATO: I'm not teasing. For after all, only a witch should be afraid of witch-hunting. For the rest of the community, it is a delightful sport.

EU: [*Curious*] How quaint? Tell me more.

ATO: I will, but first, you tell me: how were Hiawatha and Minehaha when last you met them?

EU: Now you are really teasing, Native Boy. But I thought I would learn about all these things.

ATO: [*Chuckles*] Especially witch-hunting? [*He takes her arm.*] Sorry, I don't know much about them myself. Those were only funeral drums. But I think you must have a siesta. If you don't, you'll have a nervous breakdown before you've learnt enough to graduate in primitive cultures . . .

EU: [*Looking up accusingly*] Native Boy.
[ATO *turns to look at her and sees the Coca-Cola bottle.*]

ATO: Have you been drinking Coke?

EU: Mm . . . Yes.

ATO: Excellent of you. I can't bear it warm.

EU: And of course you carried a refrigerator down here.

ATO: I am sorry.

EU: Christ, what are you apologising for? After all, I was only feeling a little homesick and I drank it for sentimental reasons. I could have had a much cooler, sweeter and more nourishing substitute in coconuts, couldn't I?

ATO: [*Confused and unable to say anything for some time*] I am thirsty too but I'll have a gin and water. [EULALIE'*s eyes follow him as he goes back to the room and she is still looking in his direction when he returns some minutes later with the*

C

bottle of gin, water and a glass. He catches the look in her eyes and sits on the terrace facing her.]

ATO: [*Mixing the drink*] Darling, what is it?

EU: What is what?

ATO: Well, there was such a look on your face. Were you going to say something?

EU: [*Gets up and moves closer to him*] Yes.

ATO: [*Lightly*] Box on then.

EU: Ato . . .

ATO: [*Interrupting*] By the way, are you interested? [*Indicating the gin and water.*]

EU: Yes.

ATO: Oh, I beg your pardon then. [*He gives her the mixture, and forgets about one for himself.*]

ATO: Aha-a.

EU: Ato, isn't it time we started a family?

ATO: [*Surprised*] Why? I thought . . .

EU: Ya, I remember I bought the idea, but I got the feeling . . .

ATO: Heavens, women! They are always getting feelings. First you got the feeling you needed a couple of years to settle down and now you are obviously getting a contradictory feeling.

EU: [*Her turn to look confused*] I hope you aren't taking it so . . . badly?

ATO: [*Boldly*] Not at all. It's only that I think we better stick to our original plans.

EU: [*Tiredly*] Okay! [*Long pause*] I'd better go and rest now.

[*She turns towards the door and the drink is entirely forgotten.* ATO *follows her into the room.*]

ACT THREE

[Six months later. Saturday afternoon. ATO *and* EULALIE *have come to spend a week-end. Her sunhat is lying on a chair in the courtyard. Two village children run in.]*

    BOY: What shall we do now?
    GIRL: *Kwaakwaa.*
    BOY: All right. I will hide, you find me.
    GIRL: No, I will not find you, I will hide.
    BOY: I say, I will hide.
    GIRL: No, I will.
    BOY: I will not allow you.
    GIRL: Then I will not play.
    BOY: If you do not, I will beat you. *[Hits her.]*
    GIRL: *[Crying]* Beast!
    BOY: Oh, I did not mean to hurt you. But you too! I have told you I want to hide . . . Let us play another game then. What shall we do?
    GIRL: Let us sing 'The Ghost'.
    BOY: Ghost . . . Ghost . . . ah, yes! *[They hold hands and skip about in circles as they sing.]*
        'One early morning,
        When the moon was up
        Shining as the sun,
        I went to Elmina Junction
        And there and there,
        I saw a wretched ghost
        Going up and down
        Singing to himself
          'Shall I go
          To Cape Coast,
          Or to Elmina
          I don't know,

I can't tell.
I don't know,
I can't tell.'

[*They repeat, but halfway through the lights go out. When the lights come up a few seconds later, the children have vanished.* ATO *bursts in immediately. His hair is dishevelled, his trousers creased and his face is looking sleepy-eyed and haggard.*]

ATO: [*Looking right and left and searching with great agitation*] Where are they? Where are those two urchins? Heavens! Those scruffy urchins and the racket of noise they were making. Why should they come here? But . . . Where are they? Or was it a dream? [*Panting*] Ugh! That's why I hate siesta. Afternoon sleep always brings me afternoon dreams, horrid, disgusting, enigmatic dreams. Damn this ghost at the junction. I loved to sing that song. Oh yes, I did. But it is all so long ago. I used to wonder what the ghost was doing there at the junction. And I used to wonder too what it did finally . . . Did it go to Elmina or to Cape Coast? And I used to wonder, oh, I used to wonder about so many things then. But why should I dream about all these things now?

[PETU *enters. He is in an old pair of trousers and a smock which make up his farm clothes.*]

Probably I am going mad?
PETU: Oh-o!
ATO: *Ei*, Uncle.
PETU: I heard you are come and that is why I am coming to greet you.
ATO: You went to the farm?
PETU: My master, where else have I to go? [*He sits on the terrace*

while ATO *still stands.*] Since the morning has found us, we must eat. And as you know, some of us are not lucky enough to be paid only to sit in an office doing nothing. And that is why I have to relieve the wayside herbs of their dew every morning.

ATO: But my Uncle, we too work hard.

PETU: [*Sarcastic*] You believe that . . . But nephew, why were you talking so hard to yourself when I came in?

ATO: [*Uneasily*] I had had a queer dream.

PETU: Is that long ago?

ATO: No. It was only this afternoon when I lay down to rest.

PETU: An afternoon dream? [*His face shows he is not terribly pleased even about the idea of it.*] What was the dream?

ATO: I dreamt that there were two children in this courtyard singing that song about the ghost who did not know whether to go to Elmina or to Cape Coast.

PETU: Ah. [*He laughs.*] How funny!

ATO: But Uncle, the boy looked like me when I was a child.

PETU: [*Serious*] Ei, this needs thinking about. Do not be disturbed, although I do not like afternoon dreams myself. I will tell your grandmother and hear what she has to say about it. [*He rises to go and sees* EULALIE's *hat.*] Did you bring your wife?

ATO: Yes. She too is resting.

PETU: [*Turns towards the door on the right*] Yo-o. I am going now. When your wife wakes up, tell her I give her welcome. I have brought some cocoyams from the farm and I will be sending her some by and by. Do not think too much about the dream.

ATO: Thank you, my Uncle. When you go, tell my mothers that we will be coming to see them this evening. [PETU *goes away.* ATO *stands confused.* EULALIE *comes in.*]

ATO: Hullo, 'Lalie.

EU: Hullo. [*They kiss each other on the cheeks.*] I heard talking here, didn't I?

ATO: My Uncle came to give us welcome.

EU: [*Anxious*] Oh, this means the whole lot of them will be coming to see us.

ATO: Would you rather we went to see the new Methodist School?

EU: Lovely. [*She kisses him on the cheek again, and takes her lovely sunhat. She puts it on and cocks her head for admiration.* ATO *says 'Exquisite' and hand in hand they come down the courtyard following the path leading to the left.*] [*Lights go off.*]

* * * *

[*Two hours later.* ESI KOM *enters from the door on the right carrying two bundles wrapped in sack cloth. She opens the door to* ATO's *apartment. She puts the bundles in the outer room, comes out and is closing the door when* ATO *and* EULALIE *enter the courtyard from the path.*]

EU: [*Sees the woman*] I say! [*She glares at* ESI KOM *for a second or two and then turns on* ATO.] Ato, would you care to ask your mother what she wants in our room?

ATO: Eh . . . Maami, were you looking for us?

ESI: Hmm . . . They told us when we arrived from the farm that you and your wife have come to spend today and tomorrow with us. So I thought I would bring you one or two things for I hear food is almost unbuyable in the city these days. And your nephews are so naughty that I knew if I did not bring them here they would steal the snails and roast them all in an hour's time.

EU: What is she saying?

ATO: Oh, she only brought us food to take back with us.

EU: What kind of food?

ATO: Maami, what did you bring?

ESI: Can not your wife herself go and see? After all, these are all women's affairs. Or do our masters, the Scholars, know what goes on in their wives' kitchen?

ATO: [*Persuasively*] Darling, will you go and check up, please?

[EULALIE *walks rather puzzled into the room. As she enters, she exclaims 'Sweet Jesus' and rushes out closing the door behind her.*]

ATO: Darling, what is it?

EU: Eh . . . some crawling things! [*Composing herself.*] Anyway, tell your mother we are very grateful.

ATO: Maami, my wife says she thanks you a lot for the things.

ESI: Tell her I am glad she likes them . . . Now, I think I will go and prepare the evening meal. Monka will cook you and your wife some rice and stew. If you need anything, you come and tell us or just shout for any of the children.

[*She turns off. Then turns back.*]

[*To* EULALIE] 'My lady', I am saying goodbye.

[*Accompanied by a wave of the hand.* EULALIE *waves back. The moment she is through the door on the right,* EULALIE *rushes to close it. Then she rushes into their room and brings out the sack bundle. She is crossing towards the path when* ATO *stops her.*]

ATO: What's all this?

EU: Those horrid creatures of course!

ATO: Where are you taking them?

EU: Throwing them away, of course.

ATO: What rubbish.

EU: What do you mean? What rubbish? If you think I am going to sleep with those creatures, then you are kidding yourself.

ATO: But how can you throw them away just like that? Haven't you seen snails before?

EU: My dear, did you see a single snail crawling on the streets of New York all the time you were in the States? And anyway, seeing snails and eating them are entirely different things!

27

[*She turns off as if to go on.* ATO *reaches her in two strides. He grabs a part of the sack.*]

ATO: But at least, I could give them to my mother to cook for me alone.

EU: And give them the opportunity to accuse me of unadaptability. No, thank you. [*She wrenches the bundle from* ATO *and as she turns off,* MONKA *opens the door on the right door. Her eyes take in the scene.* EULALIE *hurries down and dumps the sack near the path. At the same time,* MONKA *disappears closing the door on the right behind her.* EULALIE *and* ATO *just stare at each other.*]

MONKA: [*from within*] Maami, Maami, Ato's Morning Sunshine has thrown away the snails you gave them. [ATO *and* EULALIE *are still staring at each other when* ESI KOM *enters.*]

ESI: [*Addressing* ATO] Is it true that your wife has thrown away the snails I brought?

ATO: Who informed you?

ESI: That is not important, but is it true?

ATO: [*Defensively*] She does not know how to eat them . . . and . . .

ESI: And what, my son? Do you not know how to eat them now? What kind of man are you growing into? Are your wife's taboos yours? Rather your taboos should be hers.

[MONKA *re-enters and stands watching.* ATO *turns on her.*]

ATO: Yes, you went and told Maami, eh?

MONKA: Ei, take your troubles off me. Have you seen me here this afternoon?

ESI: These days, the rains are scarce and so are snails. But the one or two I get for you, you throw away.

[EULALIE *goes into their room.*]

ATO: But Eulalie . . .

MONKA: [*Derisively*] That's the golden name . . .

ESI: Yes, Hureri, Hureri . . . What does my lady say today . . .?

[EULALIE *comes back, sits on the terrace and starts puffing her cigarette.*]

MONKA: She reminds me of the words in the song:
    'She is strange,
    She is unusual.
    She would have done murder
    Had she been a man.
    But to prevent
    Such an outrage
    They made her a woman!'
Look at a female!

[EULALIE *ignores* MONKA *although her face shows she guesses at what is going on.*]

ESI: Hureri. Hmm. All the time I have been quiet as if I were a tortoise. But I have been watching, hoping that things would be different, at least, in this house.

ATO: [*Moving towards his mother*] Maami, this is only a small affair, what are you trying to say now?

ESI: What am I trying to say now?

MONKA: If nothing scratched at the palm fibre, it certainly would not have creaked.

ESI: If you listen, you will hear what I want to say. This is not the first time I have fallen into disgrace for bringing you things. Only it is my own fault. I should have learnt my lesson. The same thing happened the day I came to visit you at Accra . . .

ATO: Ah, are you still harbouring this grievance?

ESI: Do not annoy me, please. How can I forget it? I had travelled miles to come and visit you and your wife. And if

29

you threw my gifts into my face and drove me out of your house, how can I forget it?

ATO: [*In desperation*] Maami, you make me too unhappy.

ESI: Listen to what he is saying.

ATO: We asked you and Monka to stay but you insisted on coming back.

MONKA: There are two kinds of offers. One which comes right from the bowels and the other which falls from the lips only. My brother, yours fell from your lips.

ESI: I had thought I would do as other women do – spend one or two days with my daughter-in-law, teach her how to cook your favourite meals. But as if I was not noticing it, neither you nor your wife bothered to give us seats to sit on or water to cool our parched throats . . .

ATO: I remember that Monka drank water.

MONKA: I begged for it!

ESI: . . . How can I then sleep in a house where I am not welcome? . . . Where did you throw the snails? [ATO *looks left and right, uncertain of what to do.* MONKA *rushes to where* EULALIE *dumped the bundle and retrieves it.*]

MONKA: [*Coming back*] Here they are . . .

ESI: Bring them; at least we shall find a beggar to give them to. [EULALIE *makes as if to stand and speak but sits down again and continues puffing at her cigarette.*]
Oh, Esi, of the luckless soul. It is true,
Living a life of failure is like taking snuff
At the Beach. Just consider the troubles I
Have had – the school fees, the uniforms . . .

MONKA: As for the balls of *kenkey*, they are uncountable.

ESI: The tears I have shed . . .

ATO: Must you go on in that way, Maami?

ESI: Keep quiet, my son and let me speak now, for something has pricked my wound. My knees are callous with bending before the rich . . . How my friends must be laughing behind me now. 'After all the fuss, she is poorer than ever before.'

MONKA: Even I should not be such a pitiable creature now, after all, my brother is now a great man.

ESI: [*Overlapping*] Apart from the lonely journeys I made to the unsympathetic rich, how often did I weep before your Uncles and great Uncles while everyone complained that my one son's education was ruining our home.

MONKA: [*To herself*] I remember the time he was preparing to go to the white man's land where he went to take up [*indicating* EULALIE] this 'Wonder'! The money . . . the money . . . This is something which no one should hear anything about. A great part of the land was sold and even that was sufficient for nothing . . . Finally, the oldest and most valuable of the family heirlooms, *kentes* and golden ornaments, which none of us younger generation had ever seen before, were all pawned. They never brought them into daylight . . . not even to celebrate the puberty or marriage of a single girl in this house. But since our master must buy coats and trousers, they brought them out on this occasion. They were pawned, I say. And have they been redeemed? When, and with what? Ask that again.

ESI: For what do I still trouble myself, giving unacceptable gifts? . . . I cannot get a penny to pay the smallest debt I owe. Hureri must have eh . . . what do they call it?

ATO: Maami, is it not enough now? Give me time to work.

ESI: No, my son, I shall speak. You have been back a long time yet. The vulture, right from the beginning wallows in the soup he will eat. Have your Hureri got all her machines now? 'Hureri must have a *sutof*. Hureri must have something in which to put her water to cool. Hureri, Hureri. Oh, the name keeps buzzing in my head like the sting of a witch-bee! [*And with that she turns quickly off.* MONKA *turns to follow up, taking the sack with her.*]

MONKA: We are going. Ato, we wish you and your 'Morning Sun' a prosperous marriage. [*She too goes away, banging the door behind her. The couple are silent,* ATO *with a bowed head and* EULALIE *still puffing at a cigarette. Presently* ATO *speaks.*]

31

ATO: [*Quietly*] Now you have succeeded in making trouble for me. Won't you congratulate yourself? [EULALIE *continues to puff her cigarette. After what seems to be a long time, she puts the cigarette down, stamps on it, cries 'Blast' and gets up to go into the room.* ATO *comes out of the courtyard, and following the path on the left, walks ever so slowly into the night.*]

ACT FOUR

[*Another six months later. The door to* ATO's *room is open. A great deal of noise comes over from the old sector of the house. The two women are on their way from the market where they have bought fish, pig's feet, seasoned beef, etc., for their evening* fufu.]

2ND W: My sister, do not say it loudly,
   Even fish is too dear to eat these days.
1ST W: If I think I have spent
   So much on fish . . .
2ND W: And what shall I say?
1ST W: Why is there so much noise from that house today?
2ND W: Do you not know
   Tomorrow is their 'Sprinkling of the Stools'?
   The son has come from the city.
1ST W: This reminds me of something
   I had wanted to ask these many days.
   If her son gets a goodly bag by the month
   Why has Esi Kom still not . . .
2ND W: I crave pardon
   For snatching the word from your mouth.
   But my sister, roll your tobacco and stuff your pipe.
   It has not been good going,
   The roof leaks more than ever before.
1ST W: But how can it be?
2ND W: If Nakedness promises you clothes,
   Ask his name.
1ST W: But I ask, how can it be?
2ND W: You ask me?
1ST W: But you know, my sister,
   That my name is Lonesome.
   I have no one to go and listen
   To come back and tell me.

2ND W: Then scoop your ears of all their wax
And bring them here.
Esi Kom is not better than she was.

1ST W: Why?

2ND W: They never ask 'Why'.
Is it not the young man's wife?

1ST W: What has she done now?

2ND W: Listen, I hear she swallows money
As a hen does corn.

1ST W: Oh, Esi Kom!

2ND W: One must sit down
If one wants to talk of her affairs.
They say that the young man gets
No penny to buy himself a shirt . . .
But the strangest thing is that
She too works.

1ST W: Then how does she spend all that money?

2ND W: By buying cigarettes, drinks, clothes and machines.

1ST W: Machines?

2ND W: Yes, machines.
Her water must be colder than hailstone.
I heard it said in the market place
Monka's teeth were set on edge
For drinking water in her house.
And her food never knows wood fire.

1ST W: Does she tear at it uncooked?

2ND W: As for you, my sister!
She uses machines.
This woman uses machines for doing everything.

1ST W: Is that why their money
Never stays in their palms?

2ND W: But yes.

1ST W: This is very hard to understand.
Before God-up-there
My breasts have never given suck to a child,
But if what I hear mothers say are true,

Then the young people of the coming days
Are strange . . . very strange.

2ND W: Fear them, my sister.
If you meet them, jump to the wayside.
Have I not born eleven from the womb here?
I know what I am talking about.

1ST W: But this is too large for my head
Or is the wife pregnant with a machine child?

2ND W: Pregnant, with a machine child?
How can she be?
Does she know what it is to be pregnant
Even with a child of flesh and blood?

1ST W: Has she not given birth to a child since they married?

2ND W: No, my sister,
It seems as if the stranger-woman is barren.

1ST W: Barren?

2ND W: As an orange which has been scooped of all fruit?
But it is enough, my sister.

1ST W: Barren?

2ND W: One should not tell too much of a tale
And we must eat tonight.

1ST W: Barren! . . .

2ND W: I must leave you then.
You know Esi Kom's troubles are many . . .

1ST W: Barren! . . .

2ND W: The mouth will twist that says too much of them.
And as for her son's marriage,
The ear will break that hears too much of it.

1ST W: Barren!

2ND W: I say let us go. [*She takes the lead.*]

1ST W: Barren! . . .
If it is real barrenness,
Then, oh stranger-girl,
Whom I do not know,
I weep for you.
For I know what it is

35

To start a marriage with barrenness.
You ought to have kept quiet
And crouched by your mother's hearth
Wherever that is –
Yes. With your machines that cook
And your machines that sweep.
They want people.
My people have a lusty desire
To see the tender skin
On top of a child's scalp
Rise and fall with human life.
Your machines, my stranger-girl,
Cannot go on an errand
They have no hands to dress you when you are dead . . .
But you have one machine to buy now
That which will weep for you, stranger-girl
You need that most.
For my world
Which you have run to enter
Is most unkind to the barren.
And for you –
Who shall talk for the stranger?
My daughter or my sister,
Whom I have never set eyes upon,
You will cry until your throat is dry
And your eyes are blind with tears.
Yes, my young woman, I shall remember you.
I shall remember you in the hours of the night –
In my sleep,
In my sleepless sleep.

[*Lights go out.*]
[*Next morning.* PETU *enters with a wooden bowl full of white
and oiled* Oto (*mashed yam*), AKROMA *comes behind him
carrying a brass tray containing a herbal concoction and a
kind of sprinkling broom. They go round the courtyard*

sprinkling the walls and the floor first with Oto, *then with the potion. The gong man beats the gong behind them. They circle thrice round the courtyard and are just leaving when* PETU *calls to* ATO.]

PETU: Nephew!

ATO: [*Comes from the room and for the first time in cloth.*]
Here I am, my Uncle.

PETU: We have killed the goats and chickens. The women will send you and your wife some of the *Oto* and then you can eat a proper breakfast. But do you not think you and your wife should come near the Stool Rooms?

ATO: *Yoo,* Uncle. We are coming.

PETU: But you are a man. So you must come and drink with the men first.

ATO: Then I am coming with you now.
[*He goes into the room and returns in a minute. They all leave the courtyard by the door on the right.*]
[*Lights go out.*]

*　　*　　*　　*

[*Several hours later,* EULALIE *enters from the door on the right. She surveys the courtyard with disgust.*]

EU: What a blasted mess! Well. [*She shrugs her shoulders.*] I suppose folks must have their customs. Though if you ask me, I think there has been enough messing round for one day. [*She goes into the room and returns with a glass of whisky and, as usual, a packet of cigarettes and a lighter. She lights her cigarette and moving to the door on the right, peeps out into the old apartment. She makes a face.* ATO *enters from that direction.*]

EU: [*Moving to him*] Native Boy, I have missed you dreadfully.

ATO: But you left us barely five minutes ago.

EU: That shows you that after a year of marriage I am still in love with my husband which, incidentally, is a wonderful achievement.

D

ATO: By what standards? Because I am still in love with my
     wife. [*They burst out laughing.* ATO *looks down at the glass in
     her hand.*] Sweetie Pie, don't drink too much.

EU: But I have not been drinking at all.

ATO: This looks too strong.

EU: I needed it so badly. I was getting rather nervy when I
    came back.

ATO: Well, now that I am back I don't think you need it, do
     you, Sweetie Pie?

EU: Just let me finish this. [*Voices behind the door to the right.*]

ATO: I think some of my people are coming. [*Anxiously*] Let me
     put your drink in the room for you.

EU: Why?

ATO: I don't think they'll approve.

EU: [*Taking a sip*] Nonsense. [*Voices draw nearer.*]

ATO: [*Trying to take the glass from her*] But 'Lalie, don't let them
     find you in the very act.

EU: [*Sarcastically*] Is this a taboo? [*She laughs and goes into the
    room. Just then,* PETU *and* AKROMA *enter followed by*
    MONKA *carrying the brass bowl containing the herbal
    concoction. Close behind her enter* ESI KOM, MANSA,
    AKYERE *and* NANA.]

ATO: Ei!

[*He gives the two chairs in front of the door to the two men
who sit down. Everyone cries cheerfully to him* 'Afenhyiapa'.
MONKA *puts her bowl down between the two men. The
women sit round on the terrace.*]

ATO: [*Addressing* PETU] How is it I found you here, my elders.

NANA: [*From her corner*] Young man, one does not stand in ant-
      trail to pick off ants. You find somewhere to sit and then
      ask us for the purpose of the visit.

[ATO *hurries off into the room, returning with a chair on
which he sits.*]

ATO: What brings you here this afternoon?

AKROMA: Aha, now you are moving in the right path, young man.
If I am not putting my mouth into an affair which does
not concern me, may I ask you where your wife is?

NANA: Who says it is not your affair? It's his affair, isn't it?
[*Addressing this to* PETU.]

MANSA: If this isn't your affair, whose affair is it? It's everybody's
affair isn't it? [*Addressing* AKYERE.]

ESI: *Ei,* these days, one's son's marriage affair cannot   be
always be one's affair. [ATO *enters the room.*]

NANA: It may be so in many homes. Things have not changed
here. [*Knocking the ground with her stick.* ATO *returns with*
EULALIE *who shows great surprise at seeing so many people
around.*]

EU: But why so many people? [ATO *does not say anything.
Everyone just stares at her. She looks round for somewhere to
sit.* ATO *notices that and jumps up to give her his chair.*]

PETU: And where shall you sit?

ATO: Oh, there. [*Indicating a place on the terrace. Cries of*
'Ei, **Odo** *from the gathering.*]

PETU: Our master, we are going to talk to you and you must be
near enough to hear without our having to shout. [ATO
looks with consternation at EULALIE. *Their eyes meet and
they withdraw to aside where they have a tête-à-tête which is
inaudible to the audience. At the end,* EULALIE *walks away
into their room.*]

AKROMA: What has happened now?

ATO: Nothing, Uncle.

PETU: Ah, is she going away?

ATO: Eh . . . eh . . . eh . . .

AKROMA: But what we are going to say concerns her.

ATO: Eh . . . since she will not understand it, you tell me and I
will tell her everything.

NANA: I have not heard the like of this before. Is the woman for
whom stalwart men have assembled herself leaving the
place of assembly?

ESI: Yet, this is something which must not be mentioned.

PETU: And if she leaves now, whose stomach shall we wash with this medicine?

MONKA: Let us say! [*Followed by meaningful looks from the women folk.*]

ATO: Uncle, did you say you are going to use the medicine to wash my wife's stomach?

PETU: Yes.

ATO: Why?

AKROMA: Have patience, our master.

PETU: [*Looking round*] I hope I can deliver my message now.

ALL: Go on.

PETU: It was a couple of days ago that we met. What came out of the meeting is that we must come and ask you and your wife what is preventing you from giving your grandmother a great-grandchild before she leaves us. [*Everybody nods his/her head.* NANA *more violently than the others.*]

ATO: Oh!

PETU: We were to choose this day because, as you know, on this day we try to drive away all evil spirits, ill luck and unkind feelings which might have invaded our house during the past year. You know also, that we invoke our sacred dead to bring us blessings. Therefore, we are asking you to tell us what is wrong with you and your wife so that first we will wash her stomach with this, then pour the libation to ask the dead to come and remove the spirit of the evil around you and pray them to bring you a child.

ATO: [*Gripping his chair*] Good Heavens!

PETU: So my nephew, this is what we bring you. [*All eyes on* ATO.]

ATO: Oh!

AKROMA: Ato, they sent us to bring you a message and they asked us to take words from your own mouth to them. And I do not hope that you think we can go and tell them you only said 'Oh!'. What has been the cause?

ATO: Nothing . . . oh!

PETU: Haven't you got anything more to say? When two people marry, everyone expects them to have children. For men and women marry because they want children. Or I am lying, Akroma?

AKROMA: How can you be lying? It is very true.

PETU: Therefore, my nephew, if they do not have children then there is something wrong. You cannot tell us it is nothing. There is no disease in this world but it has a cure. It may cost a great deal, but money is worthless if it is not used to seek for people. If it is your wife . . .

ATO: [*Aggressively*] Why do you say it is my wife's fault?

PETU: Oh, my witness is your Uncle Akroma here. [*To* AKROMA.] Akroma, you heard me. Did I say it is his wife? All the words which came out of my mouth were 'If it is your wife . . .' How can I say it is your wife?

AKROMA: Petu could not have said that. Does he know what is in your marriage?

AKYERE: What sin would you have committed even if you said that?

ESI: I am very quiet.

AKYERE: Who does not know that she smokes cigarettes? And who has not heard that she can cut a drink as well as any man?

[*Cries of assent from all.*]

ATO: Heavens!

PETU: Nephew, we are still waiting.

AKROMA: He will say it is nothing.

PETU: What is wrong?

ATO: Nothing.

AKROMA: I told you so.

PETU: [*Angrily*] Monka, come carry the medicine. [*The women are too shocked. They stare vacantly.* MONKA *carries the brass bowl. They all stand up.*] Nephew, we will go our own way. I cannot be angry with you. I was only a messenger. Now, I remember your dream. I was going to ask the dead to come and take away the evil spirit which is haunting you. Now I know it is not a foreign evil spirit, my nephew. [*He*

41

strides out, followed by AKROMA, MONKA *and the other women.* ESI KOM *turns back and standing akimbo, stares at* ATO *for a long time. She only moves when the old woman turns back too and urges her to move, with her stick. But then she herself spits, before hobbling away.* EULALIE *peeps out and discovering that the people are gone, comes out. She paces round for some time and then walks up to* ATO. *He does not stir.*]

EU: Native Boy, what did they say? [*Silence.*]
Ato what's the matter?

ATO: They came to ask why we haven't started a family.

EU: And what did you tell them?

ATO: Nothing.

EU: What do you mean by 'nothing'? I should have thought the answer to that question is very simple.

ATO: They would say we are displeasing the spirits of our dead ancestors and the Almighty God for controlling birth . . .

EU: [*Bitterly*] You knew all this, didn't you, my gallant black knight? Now you dare not confess it before them, can you? [*She yawns*] Oh God! What an awful mess!

[*The lights go out.*]

ACT FIVE

[*The next morning. Church bells are ringing in the distance. It is Sunday.* ATO *comes in wearing a mourning cloth. He is attending the Thanksgiving Service of a cousin, fourth removed, who had died the previous year. He walks up and down, obviously irritated.*]

ATO: [*Going to the door that leads to their room*] Eulalie, how long does it take you to put on a dress? [*There is no reply. He paces up and down*] I say Eulalie am I to wait here for ever?

[*Eulalie comes in wearing a house coat. She looks very excited.*]

EU: If you must know, darling Moses, I am not coming along.
ATO: What do you mean?
EU: You know what I mean, or don't you understand English neither?
ATO: [*Turning his back to her*] I am waiting for you. If we aren't there by nine, the place will be full up and I wouldn't care to stand through a whole Thanksgiving Service.
EU: Of course, you'd only have to come back here to sleep. [*She giggles.*] I would, only I repeat 'I ain't coming' eh. Or you are too British you canna hear me Yankee lingo?
ATO: [*Miserably*] Eulalie, you've been drinking!
EU: Sure, Moses.
ATO: Again? [*In a horrified voice*] And on a Sunday morning?
EU: Poor darling Moses. Sure, I have been drinking and on a Sunday morning: How dreadful? But surely Moses, it ain't matters on which God's day a girl gets soaked, eh?
ATO: [*Anguished*] Eulalie!
EU: Yeah . . . That jus whar yar beautiful wife as com teh, Soaking on God's holy day . . . My lord, whar a morning!

43

[*Hums 'My Lord what a Morning'.*]

ATO: [*Looking tenderly at her*] Sweetie Pie.

EU: [*Laughing again*] Ain't you going teh say Poor Sweetie Pie? Ain't I poorer here as I would ave been in New York City? [*In pathetic imitation of* ATO] 'Eulalie, my people say it is not good for a woman to take alcohol. Eulalie, my people say they are not pleased to see you smoke . . . Eulalie, my people say . . . My people . . . My people . . .' Damned rotten coward of a Moses. [ATO *winces.*] I have been drinking in spite of what your people say. [*She sits on the terrace facing the audience.*] Who married me, you or your goddam people?

[*She stands and moves closer to* ATO.]

Why don't you tell them you promised me we would start having kids when I wanted them?

ATO: They won't understand.

EU: Ha! And so you make them think I am incapable of having kids to save your own face?

ATO: It isn't that.

EU: Then what is it?

ATO: They simply won't understand that one should begin having children only when one is prepared for them.

EU: Sure not. What else would they understand but their own savage customs and standards?

ATO: Eulalie!

EU: And of course, you should have known that. Have they appreciation for anything but their own prehistoric existence? More savage than dinosaurs. With their snails and their potions! You afterwards told me, didn't you, that they wanted me to strip before them and have my belly washed? Washed in that filth! [*She laughs mirthlessly.*] What did you tell them I was before you picked me, a strip-tease? . . . [*She sits down again.*] Go and weep at the funeral of a guy you never knew. These are the things they know and think are worthwhile. [*At this point, she is certainly very sober.*]

ATO: Look here. I won't have you insult . . .

EU: . . . 'My people.' Add it, Moses. I shall say anything I like. I am right tired. I must always do things to please you and your folks . . . What about the sort of things I like? Aren't they gotten any meaning on this rotten land?

ATO: [*With false forcefulness*] When in Rome, do as the Romans do.

EU: [*Contemptuously*] I thought you could do better than cliches. Since you can preach so well, can't you preach to your people to try and have just a little bit of understanding for the things they don't know anything about yet?

ATO: Shut up! How much does the American negro know?

EU: Do you compare these bastards, these stupid, narrow-minded savages with us? Do you dare . . .? [*Like the action of lightning,* ATO *smacks her on the cheek and goes out of the house going by the path on the left.* EULALIE, *stunned, holds her cheeks in her hands for several seconds. She tries to speak but the words do not come. She crumples, her body shaking violently with silent tears, into the nearest chair. This goes on for a while and then the lights go out.*]

. . . . .

[*It is midnight of the same day.* ATO *stumbles from the path into the courtyard. He can barely see his way because it is very dark. As he comes along, he cries, 'Maami, Maami,' and goes to stand behind the door on the right. The two village women, each wrapped only in a bed cloth run into the path. They are carrying little tin lamps.*]

1ST W: My sister, what is it?

2ND W: Oh, are you awake too?

1ST W: Is this noise not enough to wake the dead?
Why so much noise at midnight?

2ND W: It is very dark.
         I cannot make out the figure at the door,
         It looks like a . . . ghost.
         [*Tired*, ATO *crumples on the terrace.*]

1ST W: I think it is the son.

2ND W: Ah, you are right.

1ST W: But what does he want at this hour?

2ND W: I do not know, my sister.
         But it seems as if
         Between him and the wife
         All is not well.

1ST W: How do you know?

2ND W: Oh, I could tell you
         The bird of the Wayside
         Never tires of chirping.
         But this is no secret.
         My sons tell me this:
         On their way home
         From laying their snares
         They saw the lady wife
         Sitting on the grass in the school
         With her head bowed.

1ST W: Oh . . . And when was this, my sister?

2ND W: Just this evening.
         Darkness was approaching.

1ST W: Unlucky prophecies coming true,
         I could excel one
         Who has swallowed the dog's eye.
         . . . But what was she doing there?

2ND W: I do not know.
         And it is not part of my worries.
         Besides, marriage is like *Oware*
         Someone is bound to lose
         And another gain.

1ST W: But if both players are good,
         The game may end equally.

2ND W: And how do you know
    The players in this set are not equal?
1ST W: One has backers
    Another has not!
2ND W: People have been known to win
    Who even continue on other people's losses.
1ST W: You are right.
    And this is only the beginning.
2ND W: If we know this
    Then, my sister,
    Let us go back to mend our broken
    Sleep.

[*They leave.* ATO *gets up and starts pounding on the door again and at the same time keeps calling his mother.* ESI KOM *opens the door and comes out.* ATO *stares at her as she starts speaking.*]

ESI : *Hei,* what has happened that you wake folks from their beds? Is it very serious? Shall I go and call your uncles? Why did you and your wife not attend the Thanksgiving this morning? Where did you go? All the food we reserved for you is cold. Is it the custom of educated people not to bid goodbye when they are leaving people?

ATO: It is not that. Eulalie is gone.

ESI: [*Moving towards the front of the courtyard followed by* ATO] Where is she gone to?

ATO: I do not know.

ESI: [*Sighing*] Or is she gone to your house in the city?

ATO: I am coming from there.

ESI: Then where can she be? We thought the two of you went away together.

ATO: No.

ESI: But why should she behave in such a strange way?

ATO: I slapped her.

47

ESI: You slapped her? What did she do?

ATO: She said that my people have no understanding, that they are uncivilised.

ESI: [*Exclaims coolly and nods her head*] Is that it? [*She paces round then turns to* ATO.] My child, and why should your wife say this about us?

ATO: I do not know.

ESI: But do you never know anything? I thought those who go to school know everything . . . so your wife says we have no understanding and we are uncivilised . . . We thank her, we thank you too . . . But it would have been well if you knew why she said this.

ATO: [*Miserably*] I only asked her to come to the Thanksgiving with me. But she refused and . . .

ESI: And will she not refuse? I would have refused too if I were her. I would have known that I can always refuse to do things. [*A pause*] Her womb has receded, has it not? But did you make her know how important it is for her to . . .

ATO: But her womb has not receded!

ESI: [*Unbelieving*] What are you telling me?

ATO: If we wanted children, she would have given birth to some.

ESI: *Ei,* everyone should come and listen to this. [*She walks round in all attitudes indicating surprise.*] I have not heard anything like this before . . . Human beings deciding when they must have children? [*To* ATO] Meanwhile, where is God? [ATO *is confused since he does not know how to reply to this*] . . . yet only a woman who is barren will tell her neighbours such a tale.

ATO: But it can be done.

ESI: *Yoo,* if it can be done, do it. But I am sure any woman who does it will die by the anger of the ghosts of her fathers – or at least, she will never get the children when she wants them.

ATO: But, Maami, in these days of civilisation . . .

ESI: In these days of civilisation what? Now I know you have
been teaching your wife to insult us . . .

ATO: Oh, Maami!

ESI: Is this not the truth? Why did you not tell us that you and
your wife are gods and you can create your own children
when you want them? [ATO *is shamefaced and in spite of
wide speculations and several attempts to speak, no words
come out. There is a long pause.*] You do not even tell us
about anything and we assemble our medicines together.
While all the time your wife laughs at us because we do
not understand such things . . . yes, and she laughs at us
because we do not understand such things . . . [*Here,
mother and son face each other for a long time and it is* ATO
who is forced to look down at last.] . . . and we are angry
because we think you are both not doing what is good for
yourselves. [*She is almost addressing herself now.*] . . . and
yet who can blame her? No stranger ever breaks the law . . .
[*Another long pause.*] Hmm . . . my son. You have not dealt
with us well. And you have not dealt with your wife well in
this. [ATO *makes more futile attempts to speak.*] Tomorrow, I
will tell your grandmother, and your uncles and your
aunts about all this, and I know they will tell you that . . .
[*At this point* EULALIE *enters from the path on the right.
She is weak and looks very unhappy. She nearly crumples in
front of the courtyard while* ATO *stares dazedly at her. It is*
ESI KOM *who, following* ATO's *gaze and seeing her, rushes
forward to support her on. After a few paces into the
courtyard,* EULALIE *turns as if to speak to* ATO. *But* ESI
KOM *makes a sign to her not to say anything while she herself
continues to address* ATO . . .] . . .
Yes, and I know
They will tell you that
Before the stranger should dip his finger
Into the thick palm nut soup,
It is a townsman
Must have told him to.

And we must be careful with your wife
  You tell us her mother is dead.
If she had any tenderness,
Her ghost must be keeping watch over
All which happen to her . . .
[*There is a short silence, then clearly to* EULALIE.]
Come, my child.

[*And with that,* ESI KOM *supports* EULALIE *through the door that leads into the old house.* ATO *merely stares after them. When they finally disappear, he crosses to his own door, pauses for a second, then runs back towards the door leading to the family house, stands there for some time and finally moves to the middle of the courtyard. He looks bewildered and lost. Then suddenly, like an echo from his own mind the voices of the children break out.*]

Shall I go to Cape Coast
Shall I go to Elmina?
I can't tell
Shall I?
I can't tell
I can't tell
I can't tell
I can't tell . . .

[*The voices fade gradually out and the lights dim on him, gradually, too.*]

African Creative Writing Series

The African Creative Writing Series, under the general editorship of Professor Michael J. C. Echeruo, aims to give readers the very best in African plays, poetry and novels. The series so far includes:

EFUA T. SUTHERLAND *The Marriage of Anansewa*, a comedy about the naive and rascally attempts of Ananse to make money by betrothing his daughter to several rich chiefs simultaneously. ISBN 0 582 64139 X

UMARU LADAN and DEXTER LYNDERSAY *Shaihu Umar*, a play based on the novel by Sir Abubakar Tafawa Balewa. The Hausa hero relates the dramatic and moving story of his life while the events he describes are taking place on stage. ISBN 0 582 64192 6

OMUNJAKKO NAKIBIMBIRI *The Sobbing Sounds*, the frank and revealing 'autobiography' of an audacious young African with a lust for life. ISBN 0 582 64157 8

ISIDORE OKPEWHO *The Last Duty*, a novel set fictionally in the Nigerian Civil War, explores various attitudes to the themes of honour, conscience and self-respect.

ISBN 0 582 64622 7

AMA ATA AIDOO *Our Sister Killjoy*, or *Reflections from a Black-eyed Squint*, a running commentary of the thoughts and experiences of a Ghanaian girl travelling in the alien world of Europe. ISBN 0 582 64134 9

Other Creative Writing Already Published by Longman Includes

AMA ATA AIDOO   *No Sweetness Here*
A collection of short stories in which the author explores a variety of themes with skill and understanding.

ISBN 0 582 64037 7

PEGGY APPIAH   *A Smell of Onions*
A collection of gently humorous vignettes of life in a typical Asante village.   ISBN 0 582 64076 8

EFUA T. SUTHERLAND   *Edufa*
A play depicting how the conflict between traditional beliefs and modern circumstances forces a personal crisis upon a successful young Ghanaian.   ISBN 0 582 64029 6

AMA ATA AIDOO   *Anowa*
A play showing how a young girl who defies her parents and insists on choosing her own husband finds herself facing insurmountable problems.   ISBN 0 582 64031 8

MICHAEL J. C. ECHERUO   *Mortality*
A collection of poems by the distinguished Nigerian writer, scholar and critic.   ISBN 0 582 64033 4

JOHN PEPPER CLARK   *Casualties*
A record of the poet's reactions to the 'unspeakable events that all but tore apart Nigeria'.   ISBN 0 582 64058 X